LESS

on copyright © Summersdale Publishers Ltd, 2023
shed in 2021

eserved.

f this book may be reproduced by any means, nor transmitted,
ated into a machine language, without the written permission of
ers.

wstead has asserted her right to be identified as the author of
accordance with sections 77 and 78 of the Copyright, Designs
s Act 1988.

f Sale
sold subject to the condition that it shall not, by way of trade
e, be lent, resold, hired out or otherwise circulated in any form
r cover other than that in which it is published and without a
tion including this condition being imposed on the subsequent

UK Company
e.co.uk

imprint of Summersdale Publishers Ltd
us Publishing Group Limited
use
nbankment

dale.com

nd in China

99-081-8

ounts on bulk quantities of Summersdale books
corporations, professional associations and other
or details contact general enquiries: telephone:
7 or email: enquiries@summersdale.com.

nor the publisher can be held responsible for any loss
t of the use, or misuse, of the suggestions made herein.
ended as a substitute for the medical advice of a doctor
are experiencing problems with your physical or mental
est to follow the advice of a medical professional.

STR
LE

STRESS

This edit
First pub

All rights

No part
nor trans
the publis

Hannah B
this work in
and Patent

Condition
This book i
or otherwis
of binding
similar cond
purchaser.

An Hachette
www.hachett

Vie Books, an
Part of Octop
Carmelite Ho
50 Victoria En
LONDON
EC4Y 0DZ
UK

www.summers

Printed and bou

ISBN: 978-1-837

Substantial   dis
are   available
organizations.
+44 (0) 1243 77110

Neither the autho
or claim arising o
This book is not int
or physician. If you
health, it is always

STRESS LESS

A Little Guide to Finding Peace of Mind

HANNAH BOWSTEAD

YOU'VE
COME
SO FAR

INTRODUCTION

As our lives become increasingly busy, it may feel like stress is controlling you, rather than the other way around. If you have been feeling overwhelmed by all the thoughts in your head, even little changes can seem difficult. This book is here to help. Read on to find easy tips you can incorporate into your daily life to help you to clear your mind and stress a little less.

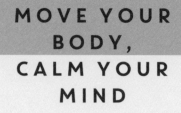

MOVE YOUR
BODY,
CALM YOUR
MIND

GET SOME
FRESH AIR

If you haven't got time for a full-on exercise session, or if you're not feeling up to it, a short walk in the open air can lift your mood no end – even if it's just for 10 minutes. Fresh air and exercise can release endorphins, which make you feel brighter and more positive. Try to find somewhere green to walk and focus on the sights, sounds and smells around you to stop yourself fixating on negative thoughts.

FIND JOY IN EVERY DAY

LAUGH IT UP

They say laughter is the best medicine, but when you're bogged down by negative thoughts it can be a struggle to get yourself to even smile. However, laughing releases endorphins – your happy hormone – which nudge you towards a better mood. Put on your favourite sitcom, watch that funny animal compilation video or simply revisit an amusing memory. A good giggle will help you relax and take your mind off things for a bit.

YOUR TODAY IS NOT YOUR FOREVER

LOOK FORWARD

Sometimes, stress and anxiety are so overwhelming that it's hard to motivate yourself to get through the day. That's why it's important to have things to look forward to. It doesn't have to be anything big – a 30-minute reading session, a slice of cake or a phone call with a friend – but that can be enough to encourage you to look beyond your stresses and keep moving forward, one day at a time.

YOU ARE IN
CONTROL

JUST BREATHE

Breathing exercises are a good way of bringing instant calm if you're feeling panicky or tense. Take ten slow, deep breaths. Visualize your feelings of worry and anxiety and release those feelings as you breathe out. It's a good idea to take 5 minutes to do this every day – perhaps first thing in the morning or during your lunch break.

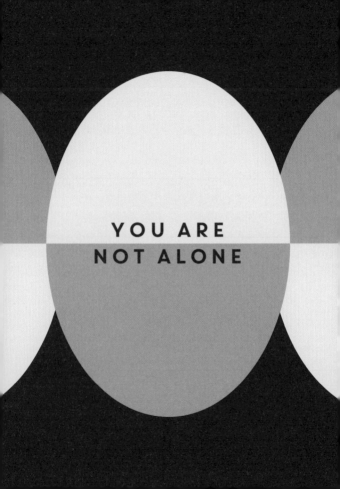

YOU ARE
NOT ALONE

JUST TALK

Although it seems like a simple thing, talking about your struggles can feel like a huge weight off your mind. Arrange to meet a trusted friend, in person over coffee or virtually. Decide in advance and let them know whether you want advice from them or whether you just want to vent! You will feel a sense of release simply by voicing your worries out loud.

THERE IS
STRENGTH
IN SILENCE

CREATE A
QUIET CORNER

Find a corner in your home to be
a relaxation zone where stress
and anxiety can't enter. Make it
cozy and inviting with blankets,
fairy lights or candles – the more
like your childhood pillow forts,
the better! When you need 15
minutes' peace, head there
with a magazine and a coffee,
or simply sit and be present.

SETBACKS LEAD TO GROWTH

FORGIVE YOURSELF

Too often, we're unnecessarily harsh on ourselves when we get things wrong, and don't give ourselves enough credit for our achievements. Remember that no one's perfect, and you're bound to make mistakes every so often. Acknowledging this is the first step to being kinder to yourself when things don't go to plan – after all, mistakes and setbacks are opportunities for learning and personal growth. You'll be stronger for it!

KEEP ON
MOVING
FORWARD

GET MOVING

Exercise really is one of the best stress-busters out there. It relieves tension, boosts your energy and concentration levels, distracts you from negative thoughts, and can even help you sleep better. Going for a jog is budget-friendly as there are no expensive gym memberships involved – all you need is a good pair of running shoes. But the most important thing is that you find an activity you enjoy, so you'll look forward to it every time!

SURROUND
YOURSELF
WITH LOVE

CHERISH YOUR FRIENDSHIPS

Even the toughest storms can be weathered with the right people by your side. But when you're at your lowest, socializing with your friends might be the last thing you want to do. Try to make the effort to reach out and spend time with your loved ones – even if it's just a simple video chat – and once you've finished putting the world to rights, you might suddenly notice that you feel a little bit better.

SMALL
STEPS LEAD
TO BIG
PROGRESS

TAKE ONE STEP
AT A TIME

Things can seem overwhelming when you're staring at the big picture or fixating on that single end goal. Thinking this way can make it impossible to get started or to get anything done. Try breaking down your goals and projects into small, manageable steps. It will no longer seem so scary to take those first few steps, and you'll start to appreciate your progress and your journey, rather than just the destination.

BREATHE IN,
RELEASE
AND LET GO

RELEASE
YOUR TENSION

If you're ever so overwhelmed that you feel like screaming, there might be a better way to let out all that pent-up frustration. Grab a piece of paper and a pen, and then scribble – just scribble – as much and as hard as you like. Don't try to make it pretty, just revel in the chaos and picture all your tension exiting your body through the pen. Then scrunch or tear up the paper and throw it away – good riddance!

CREATIVITY MAKES YOUR SOUL GROW

CREATE
SOME CALM

A creative outlet is an enjoyable way of keeping your hands busy and your mind calm. You could try taking up a new craft like knitting or crochet – there are plenty of written and video tutorials online to get you started. The repetitive stitches of knitting and crochet follow a rhythm that can be very calming, and an added bonus is the satisfaction you'll get from making something with your own hands!

GOOD
THINGS ARE
COMING

BE THANKFUL

Even in the darkest times, there are always things to be grateful for – in fact, tough times can bring these good things into sharper focus. Keep yourself anchored to the things and the people that really matter by thinking of three things you're thankful for each night before bed. This will help put your worries and anxieties into perspective. And it can't hurt to think such positive thoughts just before going to sleep!

BE THE BEST
VERSION
OF YOU

AVOID COMPARISONS

Social media can be a trigger for negative thoughts. It's all too easy to compare yourself to the perfect lives of celebrities and friends, but remember: these "perfect" lives are the carefully curated parts that these people want you to see – their own struggles and stresses are kept backstage. Try reducing the time you spend on social media if you find it too hard to stop comparing yourself to others (you can set time limits on the apps).

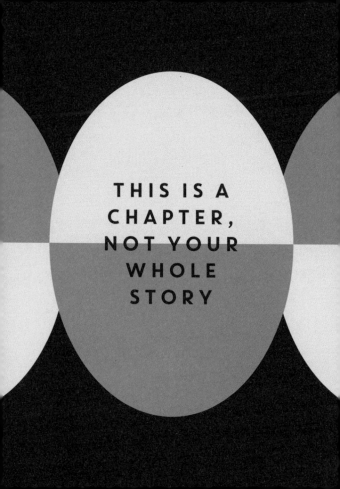

THIS IS A
CHAPTER,
NOT YOUR
WHOLE
STORY

FIND AN ESCAPE

Sometimes you just need to escape to a different world, and there's nothing quite like a good book to whisk you away from your worries for a while. Settle down in your cosiest spot, put on a calming playlist and lose yourself in someone else's story. Audiobooks are an excellent option for full immersion – there are plenty of free options online to get you started.

ENJOY THE
SWEETNESS
OF LIFE

GET BAKING

Instead of salivating over the delicious creations on your favourite baking shows, why not have a go yourself? Baking and decorating something from scratch is a calming and therapeutic process – plus, you'll have a tasty treat for yourself at the end! Don't worry about getting things wrong – mistakes happen and it'll probably still turn out fine. Now isn't that a metaphor for life!

LET GO
OF WHAT
HOLDS YOU
BACK

PUT THAT PHONE DOWN

Do you often find it impossible to put your phone down, even though there's a hundred other things you should and would rather be doing? Spending too much time on our phones can make us anxious and restless, so it's important to switch off from time to time. Find a shoebox or tin to be a "phone prison", put your phone inside and challenge yourself not to open the lid for 2 hours – or even longer.

BE GENTLE
WITH
YOURSELF

SEEK SOOTHING SCENTS

Immerse yourself in a true atmosphere of calm with stress-relieving scents such as bergamot, rosemary and camomile. Essential oils are very versatile: use them to make your own diffuser oil, add them to hot water for steam inhalation, or sprinkle a few drops on the underside of your pillow to help you sleep (lavender is a good choice for this).

GUIDE
YOURSELF
TOWARDS
INNER
PEACE

OPEN YOUR EARS

Music is such a powerful tool
for framing your mindset, so find
and save playlists for different
situations and moods. If you're
feeling stressed, search for
reading playlists or acoustic
music. If you need to focus,
give video game music a try,
because it's designed to keep
you motivated without any
distracting lyrics. It's also worth
creating your own playlist of
your favourite uplifting songs
for when you're feeling low.

LET CALM
WASH OVER
YOU

WASH YOUR WORRIES AWAY

You probably already know about the soothing effects of a hot bath, but when was the last time you had one? Often we think baths are a waste of time compared to showers. But given that a bath can elevate your mood, relax your muscles and improve your sleep, it really is worth setting the time aside. Stock up on candles, bath bombs and paperbacks you don't mind getting soggy and let the warm water wash your stress away.

REST,
RECUPERATE,
RESTORE

DON'T BE
ALARMED

Buy an alarm clock! It sounds
simple, but it might help improve
your sleep and, in turn, your energy
and mood. Your phone emits blue
light which disrupts your body's
preparations for sleep and makes
it much harder for you to drift off
naturally. It's a good idea to stop
looking at your phone an hour
or two before bed, so keep your
phone out of your bedroom and
get an alarm clock instead!

FIND PEACE
IN THE
JOURNEY

IMMERSE YOURSELF

When was the last time you sat and listened to an album all the way through? Life is often so hectic that most of us just dip in and out of playlists, or listen to music while we're doing something else like cooking or exercising. Try listening to one of your favourite albums mindfully: avoid distractions and interruptions, pay close attention to the lyrics and different instruments and experience the album's journey from start to finish.

FEEL
GROUNDED
IN THE
MOMENT

EXPERIENCE
NATURE

Nature is full of quiet calm and beauty. The rustle of leaves in a soft breeze, the tranquil flow of a stream or the carefree fluttering of a butterfly – there is so much to take in and enjoy. Find a green space or park near you, and make time to go there each week to experience the calming influence of the natural world.

BE STILL,
BE SILENT,
BE AWARE

USE YOUR SENSES

Try out this simple mindfulness exercise to keep you grounded and at peace. Sit in a quiet spot and make sure you won't be distracted. Then, as you remain still and silent, focus on each of your five senses: what can you see, hear, smell, touch and taste? Turn these over in your mind for a few minutes to foster a stronger connection with your surroundings.

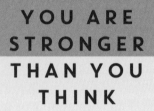

YOU ARE
STRONGER
THAN YOU
THINK

TICK IT OFF

If you ever feel like you've gone through a whole day without accomplishing anything, it might be worth writing a daily to-do list. Make sure you include small tasks like "make the bed" and "eat lunch". Factor in time for relaxing or hobbies, because self-care is just as important as – in fact, more important than – everything else! You'll soon realize that, just by making it through the day, you're achieving much more than you thought.

OPEN
YOURSELF
UP TO GOOD
THINGS

GRAB THE POPCORN

Faraway lands, daring adventures, a dash of romance… a good movie is sometimes all we need to relax of an evening. Invite your friends round and stock up on blankets and popcorn. For maximum impact, watch the cheesiest movie you can think of. The socialization and laughter will boost your spirits – and you might even enjoy the movie too!

YOU ARE
WORTHY OF
KINDNESS

TREAT YOURSELF

You deserve a spa day! Splurge on a trip to a health resort with one or two close friends, or for something a bit more budget-friendly, create your own spa at home. Foot baths and scrubs, shoulder and neck massages, and face masks and mani-pedis are all stress-relieving treatments that can be done from the comfort of your sofa.

IMPERFECTION
IS BEAUTY

EXPRESS
YOURSELF

If you are experiencing a rush
of emotions that feel as though
they will burst out of you at any
moment, you could try painting.
This can be a creative and
positive way of releasing your
anxieties or visually representing
your inner feelings. It doesn't
have to be a masterpiece!
Remember, you're painting for
yourself, not for anyone else
(unless you want others to see).

LIFE IS
TOUGH
BUT SO
ARE YOU

ENGAGE
YOUR BRAIN

Feeling restless and jittery? Keep
your fingers and your mind busy
with a puzzle or brain-teaser,
such as a crossword or sudoku.
Focusing your attention on a
single task in this way will make it
very difficult to think about anything
else and so will help restore
peace and tranquillity to your
anxious mind. This can also help
if you're struggling to fall asleep.

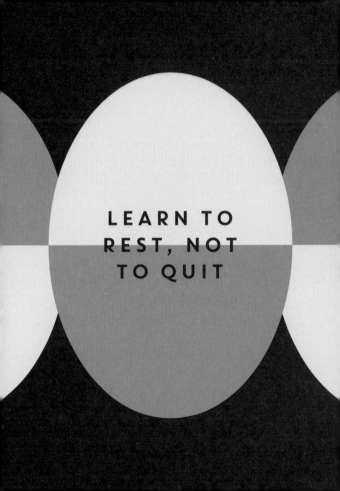

LEARN TO
REST, NOT
TO QUIT

SLEEP TIGHT

It's well known that getting regular and good quality sleep is really healthy for your mind and body, as it helps to reduce anxiety and stress. One of the keys to getting a good night's sleep is sticking to a night-time routine. Try to go to bed and wake up at the same time each day – yes, even at weekends! Wind down before bedtime with a warm bath, relaxation exercises or some reading time.

BREATHE IN
COURAGE,
EXHALE DOUBT

STRIKE A POSE

It's no secret that there are numerous mental and physical benefits to yoga. The practice is focused on breathing, strength and flexibility, and can really alleviate the effects of anxiety. Even if you are adamant that yoga isn't for you, there's no harm in giving it a go! There are plenty of online video classes if you want to try it out or you don't feel comfortable joining a class.

BE
YOURSELF,
NO MATTER
WHAT

SING IT OUT LOUD

We all have those songs that we can't help humming along to. But why just hum? Singing is a natural stress-reliever because it releases feel-good endorphins that keep you feeling uplifted. So next time you're in the shower or listening to music while you cook, give it all you've got and sing as loudly as you can. Who cares what you sound like – you're doing it for you.

GIVE
YOURSELF
PERMISSION
TO RELAX

RELAX YOUR MUSCLES

Your brain probably isn't aware of all the tension your body is holding, but progressive muscle relaxation exercises can help with that. Starting with your feet and working your way up to your face, deliberately tense each group of muscles, hold for 10 seconds, and then release, focusing on how each part of your body feels when it is totally relaxed. Over time you should learn to recognize when and where your body is holding tension.

DANCE TO YOUR OWN RHYTHM

FEEL THE BEAT

Your body is full of its own
rhythms, like the beating of
your heart and the pumping
of blood through your veins.
Externalizing these through
a rhythmic exercise, such as
tapping your feet or drumming
pencils on a surface, can help
to regulate your brain and
readjust your focus if you are
feeling stressed or scattered.

SHARE
THE GOOD
THINGS
IN LIFE

SPREAD THE LOVE

When you are kind to others,
you're actually being kind to
yourself too. Doing nice things
for your loved ones makes
you feel that warm, fuzzy glow
and, over time, strengthens the
relationships that bring you
happiness. It doesn't have to be
anything big – writing your friends
and family a simple card or letter
is a calming and fulfilling activity.

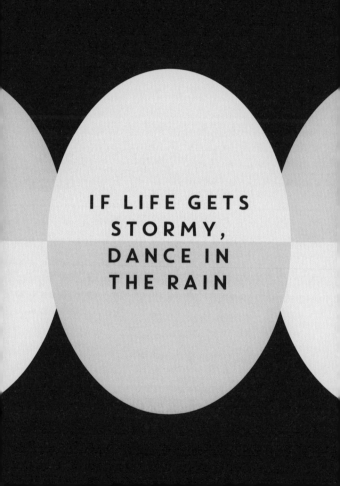

SHAKE IT OFF

Moving your body will get your heart pumping, but add in some of your favourite high-energy tunes and you'll really get those feel-good endorphins flowing. Dancing combines the stress-busting effects of exercise with the mood-lifting impact of music. So put on your favourite playlist for 20 minutes and dance like nobody's watching – they're not!

FEEL
THE PEACE
WITHIN
YOU

ENJOY A
SOOTHING DRINK

The simple pleasure of your
favourite hot beverage can lift
your mood. Take a few deep
breaths and inhale the drink's
aroma, then as you take each
sip, pay attention to the feeling of
warmth spreading through your
body. Visualize this heat releasing
all the tension from your muscles
as it goes. For a particularly
soothing drink, go for warm milk,
camomile tea or peppermint
tea just before you go to bed.

YOU ARE MORE
THAN YOUR
WORRIES

WRITE YOUR WRONGS

Our memories aren't watertight, so often we forget our past stresses and how we overcame them. Write a letter to your future self, to be opened in six months or a year from now. Pour out all the minute details of your life, your worries and how you're feeling about everything. When the future arrives and you open your letter, it'll help put your anxieties into perspective, and you might be surprised by how much progress you've made.

PRODUCTIVITY
DOES NOT
EQUAL
WORTH

DON'T FORCE IT

Society forever seems to be feeding us the message that our worth as people depends on our output or how productive we are. This is not true! You don't need to do or achieve anything to have value as a person. So go easy on yourself if you are feeling unproductive or having an off day. Accept that you are human, take a break and always prioritize your mental health.

THINK POSITIVELY

Neutralize negative and anxious thoughts by coming up with your own positive mantras to repeat loudly, either in your head or out loud. Go for something simple like "I am calm" or "I am capable", or use these cards to come up with ideas. Repeat your affirmations whenever anxious thoughts start creeping in. The more you say them, the more you will believe them!

CHALLENGE NEGATIVE THOUGHTS

Why is it that negative and anxious thoughts are always the loudest in our heads? They're difficult to ignore, but it's important to remember that thoughts are not facts. When these thoughts strike, challenge them like you would a politician you disagree with, and ask yourself why it is you're thinking this way. Then flip the negative on its head and turn it into something positive.

APPRECIATE
THE SMALL
THINGS

EAT MINDFULLY

How often do you give yourself
a proper meal break, without
trying to multitask and do
something else at the same time?
Eat your next meal mindfully,
without any distractions (the
next episode of that show can
wait!), and pay close attention to
the appearance, smell, texture
and taste of each mouthful.
You'll appreciate your food
more, and the break will give
your brain a chance to reset.

SELF-CARE
IS NOT
SELFISH

SET BOUNDARIES

Too often, we're encouraged
to view our free time as a luxury,
but taking time for ourselves is
a crucial element of self-care.
Set boundaries between work
and rest, and stick to them.
Make sure you allow yourself
to take regular breaks and time
off – you don't have to be doing
something 100 per cent of the
time! Remember: never feel
guilty for taking care of yourself.

MAKE ROOM
FOR PEACE

TIDY DESK, TIDY MIND

Is your workspace a place where you feel comfortable, relaxed and motivated? If not, it might be time for a declutter. Clear away all the unnecessary stuff that's accumulated on your desk and get some storage baskets for the things you really need. Add a couple of personal items like photos to make you smile. Having a tidy desk will aid your focus and create a calming environment in which to work.

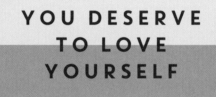

YOU DESERVE
TO LOVE
YOURSELF

KNOW THE SIGNS

Sometimes, a headache is just a headache. But sometimes it's a sign that you're more stressed than you think. Be aware of the physical symptoms of stress – things like insomnia, fatigue and irritability – this is your body trying to tell you to slow down! Once you can recognize your body's signs and signals, you can begin to do something about your stress.

CALM IS A
SUPERPOWER

TACKLE IT
HEAD ON

Ignore it and it'll go away.
How many times have we told
ourselves that? But ignoring
your stressors will only make
them stronger. Confront your
stressors: recognize what
they are, acknowledge their
existence, and if a stressor can
be changed or removed from
your life, take steps to do just
that. If there are stressors which
can't be removed, such as work
or family, you can at least plan
for how to cope with them.

KEEP GOING
AND SEE
WHAT
HAPPENS

STAND UP

Nowadays, many of us spend most of our day sitting still, but this isn't great for our bodies or our minds! If your routine sees you sitting down for long periods of time, try to get up for just a couple of minutes every half hour. This will get your muscles moving and improve your blood circulation, and it will give your brain a bit of a break to avoid too much stress building up.

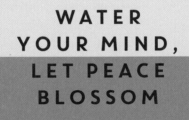

WATER
YOUR MIND,
LET PEACE
BLOSSOM

DRINK UP

Are you drinking enough water? Our bodies are made up of roughly 60 per cent water, so think of it as the fuel that keeps your body going. Water is essential for many different reasons, including keeping your brain functioning properly, but high stress levels can lead to dehydration. That's why it's so important to drink plenty and often!

NOURISH YOURSELF AND YOU'LL GROW

PLANT POSITIVITY

If you can't go outdoors, bring the outdoors to you! Houseplants are excellent roommates as they can boost your mood and productivity and improve the air quality of your home, helping to alleviate the symptoms of stress and anxiety. Time spent tending to and nourishing your plant babies can also be therapeutic, rewarding and, above all, incredibly calming.

IF IT
WEIGHS
YOU DOWN,
LET IT GO

DECLUTTER
YOUR DEVICES

So you've taken 10,000 photos on your phone – but when did you last look at any of them? Take an hour, put on some music or a podcast, and go through all your photos. There's probably some memories you've forgotten about! Delete all those multiples you don't need, and if you want to go one step further, print some pics out (gasp!) and make a photo album.

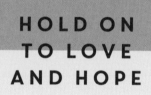

HOLD ON
TO LOVE
AND HOPE

CHOOSE A
LUCKY CHARM

Find a small object – something
you can hold in your hand like
a piece of jewellery or a button
– that can be your talisman.
Choose something that's
significant to you: perhaps it
reminds you of a loved one or a
special event in your life. Always
keep it in your pocket or bag,
and hold it in your hand when you
need to feel calm and grounded.

GIVE
YOURSELF
SPACE TO
BREATHE

GET ORGANIZED

It's amazing how much brighter and clearer our minds feel when our environment is tidy and welcoming. Cleaning and decluttering may not be your favourite thing to do, but you will feel a whole lot better once it's done. Focus on one room or area instead of trying to do everything in one go. Plus, now is your excuse to get some attractive storage boxes and baskets to keep everything in place.

MAKE TIME
FOR THE
THINGS
THAT
MATTER

GO SCREEN-FREE

If you're thinking that you don't have time to try any of these stress-busting ideas, why not plan a digital-free weekend? Switch off your TV, laptop and phone (except for emergencies!). If it's summer, go for a relaxing bike ride or picnic. If it's cold, curl up with a cosy craft or board game. Enjoy this precious time saved by not scrolling through social media. If it's a success, you can try it every month!

FILL YOUR
HEART WITH
CURIOSITY

GET OUT OF
THE HOUSE

How well do you know the secrets
of your local area? When you
need a change of environment,
go exploring and venture away
from the main roads. You might
stumble upon some hidden gems,
like a cosy pub or coffee shop
where you can work for a couple
of hours, or a quiet bookshop
where you can find sanctuary
and a few minutes' peace.

BELIEVE
THAT
EVERYTHING
WILL WORK
OUT

LET IT GO

A lot of anxiety stems from feeling a lack of control. We always want to be in the driver's seat and can feel uneasy when we're not. Try to accept the things you can't change – there's no point worrying about them! Let go of your controlling urge and enjoy the peace that comes from freeing up all that space in your mind. Remember, while you can't always control what happens, you can control how you respond.

TAKE EACH
DAY AS IT
COMES

LEARN TO
MONOTASK

Multitasking is your enemy when you're trying to maintain a calm mind. Flitting between your email inbox, that big report and your notes for the meeting might make you feel more productive, but how can your brain get anything done when it's constantly switching between tasks? Focus on one job at a time and give your full attention to it. You'll probably find that you get loads more done, and feel less stressed to boot.

FORGET
ABOUT THE
WORLD FOR
NOW

LOSE YOURSELF

Make use of the tranquil spaces in your local area. Put aside a few hours one weekend to visit a library or museum and soak up the quiet, calming atmosphere. These are usually excellent places to get lost in – literally and figuratively – and you'll probably find yourself learning something too. You'll have the added bonus of feeling really cultured!

TAKE TIME
TO RECHARGE
AND HEAL

TAKE A BREAK

If you've tried lots of these tips and nothing makes you feel better, it might be time for a weekend away. You could go abroad, or stay somewhere closer to home if you want to keep costs down (camping is a great option!). Just a couple of days away from your normal life and all its stresses will help to reset and replenish your mind. Try not to plan too much to do – see where the mood takes you!

YOU ARE
SURROUNDED
BY LOVE

HUG IT OUT

A simple hug is a powerful medicine for reducing stress and anxiety. That's because hugging – and the social bonding that comes with it – stimulates your brain to release a feel-good hormone called oxytocin, which makes us feel comforted and calm. In fact, it's even sometimes called the "cuddle hormone"! So find a friend, family member or your significant other and give them a giant bear hug pronto!

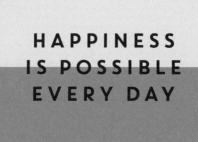

HAPPINESS
IS POSSIBLE
EVERY DAY

CAPTURE YOUR MEMORIES

With the rise of smartphones and social media, fewer and fewer of us are recording our memories in physical form, but creating a memory scrapbook can be a calming and mindful process. Instead of throwing them away, collect tickets and memorabilia from events and arrange them in a notebook with photos and bits of writing. Looking back through the scrapbook will also bring you peace and happiness!

RELEASE
STRESS AND
INVITE
CALM

KEEP YOUR HANDS BUSY

Do you often find yourself wringing your hands or picking at your fingers when you're stressed or nervous? Find yourself something to fidget with to keep your hands busy. Most people find popping bubble wrap or squishing play dough to be calming and satisfying. Alternatively, search online for a fidget toy: there are loads of products that have been designed for this purpose.

YOU CAN
CREATE
YOUR OWN
CALM

MAKE TIME
FOR MAKING

Give your stress an outlet by
taking up a new calming hobby.
Cooking, writing, woodworking or
embroidery – whatever takes your
fancy, find a class near you or look
for an online tutorial and give it a
go. Doing something creative is a
tried-and-tested way of relieving
stress and focusing the mind, and
there is so much joy to be found in
the process of creating. You might
make some new friends too!

CHOOSE
HAPPINESS
IN THIS
MOMENT

FIND A PET PAL

If you have a dog or cat, you'll be well aware of just how good it feels to give them a good hug or scratch. If your lifestyle or living arrangements mean you can't have a pet, ask if you can hang out with a friend's pet for an hour or two (and let your friend know you're available for dog- or cat-sitting). Your new four-legged bestie will calm you down in no time.

PRIORITIZE
YOUR
HAPPINESS

JUST SAY NO

If you often feel pressured
into saying yes to things you
don't really want or have the
time to do, you're not alone.
It's understandable – you don't
want your friends to think you're
antisocial or your colleagues to
think you're lazy. But cramming
everything into your schedule
will only make you stressed
and burned-out. Learn to
say no from time to time and
prioritize your well-being – good
friends will totally understand!

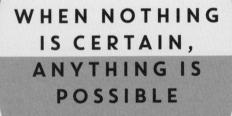

WHEN NOTHING
IS CERTAIN,
ANYTHING IS
POSSIBLE

DO SOMETHING DARING

Sometimes you just want to curl up and watch sitcoms all day – and that's fine – but it's good to get outside your comfort zone too. Consider taking up a new hobby – something that's totally different from anything else you do, like horse riding or archery (or why not both at the same time!). You might find that doing something nerve-wracking helps you manage your worries and fears, and you'll gain bucket-loads of confidence as well!

EACH DAY IS AN OPPORTUNITY

GET INVOLVED

What's happening in your local area? Is there a farmers' market every Saturday, a flea market once a month or a summer festival? Find out! Getting involved in local events will help you feel grounded and rooted in your community, so go out and enjoy the carefree feeling you'll get from forgetting about your worries for a few hours.

TODAY
WILL BE
A GOOD
DAY

GET UP AND GET GOING

Most people find it difficult to get in enough exercise during the week. There's not enough time! But, if you can, one great way of fitting in more exercise is to walk or cycle part or all of your commute. You could park further away from your workplace, or catch the bus two stops on from your usual one. The early-morning exercise will put you in a positive frame of mind for the day ahead.

CELEBRATE
YOUR
INDIVIDUALITY

BE YOUR OWN
BIGGEST FAN

When you've made a mistake, do you find yourself going over it again and again in your head, analyzing every tiny detail? Stop torturing yourself! You've probably never obsessed over your achievements in quite the same way. Next time you catch yourself fixating on something that hasn't gone to plan, put one of your successes on repeat instead, focusing on your strengths and just how awesome you are.

LOVE THE
LIFE YOU
HAVE

LIVE WITH LESS

In today's world, we're constantly
pressured to buy and own more
things, be it technology, clothing
or gifts. The constant urge to buy
the latest version or the newest
"big thing" is not only exhausting,
but stressful and ultimately
unfulfilling. Embrace what
you already have and learn
to be content – otherwise
you'll never be satisfied!

ACCEPT
YOURSELF
FOR WHO
YOU ARE

STOP PRETENDING

Pretending to be fine when you're most definitely not is one of the most exhausting things in the world. But do you know what? It's OK not to be OK. Everyone goes through tough times and you don't have to be upbeat and cheerful 100 per cent of the time. Your friends will understand and may even be able to help. So give yourself a break – your tired brain will thank you for it.

LOVE
YOURSELF
AS YOU
LOVE
OTHERS

BE KIND TO YOURSELF

Would you tell your best friend that they're stupid, that they're a failure and will never achieve anything? Of course not! So why do you say these things to yourself? Respond to yourself the way you would to a friend if they told you they were a waste of space. Treat yourself with the kindness and respect that you deserve!

PRIORITIZE
THOSE WHO
PRIORITIZE
YOU

STREAMLINE YOUR FEED

Do you have dozens of social media "friends" that you haven't seen in years? Are there people you follow online that stress you out or rub you up the wrong way? If you answered "yes" to both questions, then it might be time to have a digital detox and mute, unfollow or block the people whose content is no longer relevant to you. Your new, streamlined social media feeds will be so much more calming!

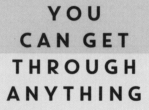

YOU
CAN GET
THROUGH
ANYTHING

BE PREPARED

If there's a big, stressful event looming on the horizon, one of the best ways to reduce your stress is to make sure you plan well in advance. Do you need to make a long journey? Book and double check your travel arrangements. Do you have to speak in public? Write the speech early and practise with a friend. Being properly prepared will help you manage the rising feelings of anxiety.

DRESS
YOURSELF
IN HOPE AND
KINDNESS

HAVE A CLOSET
CLEAR-OUT

If we're honest with ourselves, we
all probably have more clothes
than we need. Luckily, decluttering
and rearranging your wardrobe is
an effective de-stressing activity.
Consider donating anything you
haven't worn in the last year, and
finally do all those repairs you've
been putting off for months! Sort
your wardrobe by clothing type or
category (workwear, loungewear,
active wear), then bask in that
calm feeling of accomplishment.

YOU ARE
CAPABLE

BALANCE
YOUR BUDGET

Money is one of the top causes of stress. If you're constantly worrying about next month's outgoings, make sure you're keeping (and regularly updating) a budget. Once you've tracked your spending in different categories (groceries, travel, hobbies, eating out and so on) you can identify areas where you might be able to save money. Keeping on top of your finances will minimize those anxious feelings of spiralling out of control.

EVERY
DAY YOU
GROW MORE
RESILIENT

EAT HEALTHILY

Give your body a fighting chance when it comes to dealing with stress. This might sound like basic stuff, but eating a balanced diet, with three meals a day and plenty of fruit and vegetables, is going to give your body the fuel it needs to manage times of anxiety. Try to avoid snacking on the sugary foods you crave when you're stressed, and opt for fruit or nuts instead. You'll soon be bursting with positive energy!

YOU ARE
ENOUGH,
RIGHT NOW

TAKE IT EASY

You might be thinking, "How can I possibly introduce so many changes in one go? Not being stressed is so stressful!" But trying to do everything in one go is going to lead to burnout – just pick one or two things! And it's important to remember that you are not a failure because you don't go for a run five times a week or didn't eat a single vegetable today. In fact, you're not a failure – full stop.

Have you enjoyed this book?
If so, find us on Facebook at
Summersdale Publishers, on
Twitter at **@Summersdale**
and on Instagram and TikTok at
@summersdalebooks and get in
touch. We'd love to hear from you!

www.summersdale.com